THINK BIG, GROW BIGGER

Mastering the Entrepreneurial Mindset

THINK BIG, GROW BIGGER

Mastering the Entrepreneurial Mindset

SAMUEL THEO YAMTHE

Think Big, Grow Bigger:
Mastering the Entrepreneurial Mindset
Samuel Theo Yamthe

ISBN: 979-8-89705-364-3.

TABLE OF CONTENTS

Chapter 1: Introduction to the Entrepreneurial Mindset

THE IMPORTANCE OF MINDSET IN BUSINESS

The mindset of an entrepreneur plays a critical role in determining the success of a business. It encompasses the beliefs, attitudes, and thought patterns that shape business owners' approach to challenges, opportunities, and daily operations. Adopting a growth-oriented mindset enables entrepreneurs to navigate the inevitable ups and downs of running a business. This perspective fosters resilience in the face of adversity and encourages continuous learning and adaptation, which are essential for long-term success.

A growth mindset allows entrepreneurs to view failures as valuable learning experiences rather than insurmountable obstacles. This shift in perspective is crucial, as the entrepreneurship journey is often fraught with setbacks. By embracing failure as a component of the learning process, business owners can extract insights from their experiences, rethink their strategies, and ultimately improve their decision-making. This proactive approach to challenges can differentiate successful entrepreneurs from those who may give up in the face of difficulties.

Moreover, a positive mindset enhances an entrepreneur's ability to inspire and lead their teams. Employees are more likely to feel motivated and engaged when they perceive their leaders as optimistic and forward-thinking. A mindset emphasizing collaboration, innovation, and open communication fosters a supportive work environment where team members feel valued and empowered. This culture not only boosts morale but also drives productivity, ultimately contributing to the overall growth of the business.

Additionally, mindset influences how entrepreneurs set and pursue their goals. Those with a strong entrepreneurial mindset are likelier to set ambitious yet attainable objectives, pushing the boundaries of what is possible. They tend to embrace risk and uncertainty, viewing them as integral to the entrepreneurial journey. This willingness to step outside their comfort zones can lead to innovative solutions and new opportunities, propelling their businesses to greater heights.

In conclusion, cultivating the right mindset is essential for small business owners and entrepreneurs seeking growth and success. By fostering a growth-oriented perspective, embracing failure, leading with positivity, and setting ambitious goals, entrepreneurs can successfully navigate the complexities of business. Ultimately, the mindset adopted by business owners not only shapes their paths but also significantly impacts the culture and success of their businesses.

CHARACTERISTICS OF A GROWTH-ORIENTED MINDSET

A growth-oriented mindset is characterized by a deep-rooted belief that abilities and intelligence can be developed through dedication and hard work. This perspective fosters a love for learning and resilience essential for overcoming challenges. Small business owners and entrepreneurs with a growth mindset view failures not as setbacks but as opportunities for growth and development. This attitude enables them to embrace challenges, persist in the face of setbacks, and see effort as a path to mastery, ultimately driving their businesses toward success.

Embracing challenges is a hallmark of a growth-oriented mindset. Entrepreneurs often encounter obstacles that test their resolve and adaptability. Those who adopt a growth mindset welcome these challenges, understanding that they are essential for personal and professional development. By stepping outside their comfort zones, they expand their skills and gain valuable insights to inform their business strategies. This willingness to tackle difficult situations head-on enables small business owners to innovate and stay competitive in an ever-evolving marketplace.

Another key characteristic of a growth-oriented mindset is the emphasis on learning from feedback. Constructive criticism is viewed as a valuable resource rather than a personal attack. Entrepreneurs with this mindset actively seek feedback from customers, peers, and mentors to renew their business practices and offerings. This openness to learning fosters a culture of continuous improvement, allowing small business owners to adapt to changing market conditions and better meet the needs of their customers, ultimately positioning themselves for sustained growth.

Persistence is a vital trait associated with a growth-oriented mindset. Entrepreneurs often face numerous challenges, and those who cultivate resilience are likelier to persevere through difficult times. This persistence is fueled by the belief that effort and hard work can produce meaningful results. Small business owners can navigate setbacks without losing sight of their vision by focusing on their long-term goals. This relentless pursuit of growth motivates the individual and inspires their teams, creating a united front in the quest for success.

Finally, a growth-oriented mindset encourages collaboration and the sharing of knowledge. Entrepreneurs who adopt this perspective understand that learning from others is as essential as individual growth. They actively seek partnerships and build networks that facilitate the exchange of ideas and resources. This collaborative approach enhances creativity, drives innovation, and fosters a community of support among small business owners. By leveraging collective strengths, entrepreneurs can accelerate their growth and contribute positively to their industries, creating a ripple effect of progress and development.

OVERCOMING LIMITING BELIEFS

Overcoming limiting beliefs is crucial for small business owners and entrepreneurs who aspire to reach new heights in their ventures. Limiting beliefs are the internal narratives that often stem from experiences, societal expectations, or self-doubt. These beliefs can create barriers that inhibit growth and creativity and prevent individuals from seizing opportunities. Recognizing and challenging these beliefs is essential for fostering a mindset conducive to success and innovation.

The first step in overcoming limiting beliefs is to identify them. Entrepreneurs must self-evaluate to uncover the thoughts that undermine their competence and potential. Common limiting beliefs include thoughts like "I'm not qualified enough," "I can't compete with larger companies," or "Success is only for a select few." By acknowledging these thoughts, business owners can begin to dissect their origins and understand how they influence decision-making and behavior. This process of self-discovery allows individuals to confront their fears and uncertainties directly, paving the way for transformation.

Once limiting beliefs have been identified, entrepreneurs can work on reframing them. This involves challenging the validity of these beliefs and replacing them with empowering affirmations. For instance, instead of thinking, "I am not capable," one might reframe it as "I have unique skills that can contribute to my success." Consistent reframing must be consistently practiced, as repetition helps solidify new, positive beliefs. Visualization techniques, journaling, and positive self-talk can reinforce this new mindset, enabling entrepreneurs to cultivate resilience and confidence.

Another effective strategy for overcoming limiting beliefs is seeking support from a like-minded community. Networking with other entrepreneurs can provide valuable insights and encouragement. Sharing experiences and challenges with peers fosters an environment where individuals feel less isolated in their struggles. Additionally, mentorship can offer guidance and perspective, helping entrepreneurs see that others have faced similar doubts and successfully navigated through them. This communal support can serve as a potent reminder that overcoming limiting beliefs is a shared journey.

Finally, embracing a growth mindset is essential in overcoming limiting beliefs. Entrepreneurs should view challenges as opportunities for learning and growth rather than insurmountable obstacles. Business owners can cultivate resilience and adaptability by prioritizing development over perfection. This perspective encourages experimentation and innovation, allowing entrepreneurs to take calculated risks that propel their businesses forward. In this way, overcoming limiting beliefs becomes a personal endeavor and a foundational aspect of a thriving entrepreneurial mindset, ultimately driving growth and success.

Chapter 2: Defining Your Vision

CRAFTING A COMPELLING BUSINESS VISION

A compelling business vision serves as the foundation for any successful enterprise. It is a guiding star that directs a business owner's and their team's actions and decisions. When crafting a vision, it is essential to articulate a clear and inspiring picture of the future that the business aims to achieve. This vision should resonate with the entrepreneur's aspirations and the organization's broader goals. It must encapsulate the essence of what the business stands for, providing a sense of purpose that motivates all stakeholders involved.

To begin the process of crafting a compelling vision, entrepreneurs should engage in deep reflection on their core values and long-term aspirations. This involves asking critical questions such as: What impact do I want my business to have on my community? What legacy do I wish to leave behind? By exploring these questions, business owners can identify the driving forces behind their entrepreneurial journey. This introspective approach ensures that the vision is not only aspirational but also authentic, reflecting the true character and ambition of the entrepreneur.

Once the foundational elements are in place, it is crucial to translate these insights into a succinct and memorable vision statement. A well-crafted vision statement should be clear, concise, and easy to communicate. It should evoke emotion and inspire action, serving as a rallying cry for employees, customers, and stakeholders. Utilizing vivid imagery and powerful language can enhance the statement's effectiveness, making it more relatable and engaging. Additionally, incorporating specific goals or milestones can provide a tangible framework for measuring progress toward achieving the vision.

The process of communicating the vision is just as important as its creation. Entrepreneurs must actively share their vision with their team and ensure it permeates the company culture. This can be achieved through regular discussions, team meetings, and visual representations in the workplace. When employees understand and embrace the vision, they are more likely to align their efforts with the business's overarching goals. This alignment fosters a sense of ownership and accountability, encouraging team members to contribute proactively to the vision's realization.

Finally, a compelling business vision is not static; it requires ongoing evaluation and adaptation. As markets evolve and new challenges arise, entrepreneurs should revisit their vision to ensure its relevance and effectiveness. Gathering feedback from employees and stakeholders can provide valuable insights into how the vision resonates with others. By remaining flexible and open to change, business owners can rene their vision to better align with their evolving goals and customers' needs. In doing so, they strengthen their business and solidify their position as leaders in their respective industries.

ALIGNING VISION WITH VALUES

Aligning vision with values is critical for small business owners and entrepreneurs seeking sustainable growth. A clear vision provides direction and purpose, while values serve as the foundation upon which decisions are made and actions are taken. When these two elements are harmonized, they create a coherent narrative that guides daily operations, inspires employees, attracts customers, and fosters loyalty. Entrepreneurs must take the time to define their vision and articulate their values to ensure they are working towards a common goal.

The vision of a business encapsulates what the owner aspires to achieve in the long term. It is a forward-looking statement that paints a picture of success and is a motivational force. However, it can become a hollow aspiration without values to support this vision. Values are the principles and ethics that guide behavior and decision-making within the organization. They embody what the entrepreneur stands for and what the company represents. By identifying and integrating core values into the vision, entrepreneurs can cultivate a strong organizational culture that aligns with their strategic goals.

One effective method for aligning vision with values is through stakeholder engagement. Business owners should involve employees, customers, and other stakeholders in discussing the company's vision and values. This collaborative approach enriches the vision with diverse perspectives and fosters a sense of ownership among stakeholders. When employees feel that their input is valued, they are more likely to buy into the vision and embody the values, leading to enhanced motivation and productivity.

Moreover, regular reflection and reassessment are essential for maintaining alignment between vision and values. As businesses evolve, their environments change, and new challenges arise. Entrepreneurs should be proactive in evaluating whether their vision and values still resonate with their current objectives and market realities. This might involve soliciting feedback, conducting surveys, or holding workshops to ensure the organization remains aligned with its foundational beliefs. By being adaptable, entrepreneurs can pivot their strategies while staying true to their core principles.

Ultimately, aligning vision with values is not a one-time task but an ongoing process that requires commitment and diligence. Small business owners and entrepreneurs must continuously communicate their vision and values to all stakeholders, reinforcing their importance in every aspect of the business. This alignment strengthens the internal culture and enhances external perceptions of the brand. When a company operates with a clear vision rooted in strong values, it is better positioned to achieve long-term growth and success in an increasingly competitive marketplace.

COMMUNICATING YOUR VISION EFFECTIVELY

Communicating your vision effectively is critical for small business owners and entrepreneurs who aspire to grow their enterprises. A clear, compelling vision is the foundation for your business strategy, guiding decisions and inspiring your team. To convey your vision, you must first articulate it in a way that resonates with your audience. This involves not only defining your goals and values but also presenting them in a relatable manner. Use simple, straightforward language that avoids jargon, ensuring that everyone involved understands the purpose and direction of your business.

Once you have articulated your vision, the next step is to ensure consistency in communicating it across all platforms and interactions. Whether through marketing materials, team meetings, or social media channels, maintaining a consistent message reinforces your vision and helps to build brand identity. This consistency fosters trust among stakeholders and creates a unique narrative that your audience can rally around. Frequent repetition of your vision in various forms will help embed it in the minds of your employees and customers, making it a part of your company's culture.

Engaging storytelling is another powerful tool for communicating your vision. People are naturally drawn to stories; weaving your vision into a narrative can make it more compelling and memorable. Share personal anecdotes or experiences that inspired your vision, and illustrate how it translates into real-world impact. This narrative approach humanizes your business and connects emotionally with your audience, encouraging them to invest in your vision. When your team and customers feel emotionally connected to your story, they are more likely to support and advocate for your business.

Feedback mechanisms are essential for effective communication of your vision. Encourage open dialogue with your employees and stakeholders to understand their perceptions and interpretations of your vision. This can be achieved through surveys, one-on-one discussions, or team workshops. By actively seeking feedback, you demonstrate that you value their input, which can lead to greater buy-in and commitment to your vision. Additionally, incorporating feedback can help reinforce your message and ensure that it aligns with your team's and customers' expectations and aspirations.

Finally, leading by example is crucial in reinforcing your vision. As a business owner or entrepreneur, your actions should reflect the values and goals you promote. Consistently demonstrate commitment to your vision through your decisions and behavior, setting a standard for your team to follow. When employees see you embodying the vision, they are more likely to adopt it themselves. This alignment not only cultivates a motivated workforce but also creates a strong organizational culture that supports growth and innovation, ultimately driving your business toward success.

Chapter 3: Setting Goals for Growth

THE SMART GOALS FRAMEWORK

The SMART Goals Framework is an essential tool for small business owners and entrepreneurs aiming to cultivate a mindset geared toward growth and success. This framework emphasizes the importance of setting specific, Measurable, Achievable, Relevant, and Time-bound goals. By applying the SMART criteria, entrepreneurs can create a clear roadmap that guides their strategic planning and enhances their ability to track progress and make necessary adjustments along the way.

Specificity is the first pillar of the SMART framework. Goals should be unambiguous, clearly detailing what you want to achieve. For instance, instead of stating a vague goal like "increase sales," a specific goal would articulate the exact percentage increase in sales you aim to achieve within a de ned period. This clarity prevents misunderstandings and keeps the team focused on the essential tasks contributing to the overall objective. By narrowing the focus, entrepreneurs can allocate resources more effectively and ensure that every team member understands their role in reaching the goal.

Measurability is the second component, which allows entrepreneurs to assess progress quantitatively. By using measurable criteria for success, business owners can track their achievements and determine what strategies are working or need adjustment. This might involve setting numerical targets, such as a specific revenue gain or the number of new customers acquired. Regularly reviewing these metrics motivates the team and provides valuable insights into the effectiveness of various initiatives, fostering a culture of accountability and continuous improvement.

Achievability ensures that goals are realistic and attainable, considering the resources available and the business's current circumstances. While setting ambitious targets that encourage growth is essential, they must also be grounded in reality. Setting unattainable goals can lead to frustration and demotivation among team members. Entrepreneurs should assess their capabilities, market conditions, and potential obstacles when formulating these goals. This balance between aspiration and realism fosters a more resilient entrepreneurial mindset as business owners learn to navigate challenges without losing sight of their vision.

Goals should align with the broader objectives of the business, ensuring that every effort contributes to long-term success. This connection reinforces the importance of each goal, helping entrepreneurs prioritize their activities effectively. Furthermore, establishing a timeline creates a sense of urgency and encourages consistent effort toward goal completion. By setting deadlines, entrepreneurs can better manage their time and resources, fostering a proactive approach to growth that propels the business forward. Implementing the SMART Goals Framework empowers small business owners to think strategically, embrace challenges, and achieve sustainable development.

SHORT-TERM VS. LONG-TERM GOALS

Setting goals is a fundamental aspect of entrepreneurship, and understanding the distinction between short-term and long-term goals can significantly impact a business's trajectory. Short-term goals typically span a few weeks to a year and are often tactical. These objectives help entrepreneurs manage daily operations, respond to immediate challenges, and seize opportunities. Small business owners can use short-term goals to enhance their decision-making processes, allocate resources efficiently, and measure progress. By focusing on attainable milestones, entrepreneurs can maintain motivation and create a sense of accomplishment that fuels further ambition.

On the other hand, long-term goals are more strategic, extending beyond one year and often envisioning the future of the business over several years or even decades. These goals are the overarching mission and vision of the company. They provide a framework for the business's goals, guiding major decisions and resource investments. For small business owners, articulating long-term goals is essential for building a sustainable competitive advantage. These objectives include expanding into new markets, developing innovative products, or creating a strong brand identity. The clarity provided by long-term goals helps entrepreneurs align their short-term actions with their broader aspirations.

Balancing short-term and long-term goals is crucial for sustainable growth. While short-term goals enable entrepreneurs to respond to immediate needs, they should not overshadow the larger vision. Small business owners must ensure their daily activities contribute to their long-term aspirations. This requires a disciplined approach to goal-setting, where entrepreneurs regularly assess their progress and adjust their strategies as necessary. By integrating both types of goals, business owners can create a dynamic roadmap that fosters agility while keeping the bigger picture in focus.

Moreover, the entrepreneurial mindset is pivotal in how small business owners approach goal-setting. A mindset oriented towards growth encourages entrepreneurs to view challenges as opportunities and fosters resilience in the face of setbacks. When entrepreneurs adopt this mindset, they become more adept at setting realistic short-term goals that serve as stepping stones toward their long-term vision. This iterative process of setting, evaluating, and adjusting goals cultivates a culture of continuous improvement, which is essential for thriving in a competitive landscape.

Ultimately, understanding the interplay between short-term and long-term goals empowers small business owners to create a holistic strategy for growth. By recognizing the importance of both goals, entrepreneurs can develop a comprehensive framework that drives immediate results and positions their business for future success. As they navigate the complexities of entrepreneurship, a clear focus on short-term achievements and long-term aspirations will enable business owners to think big and grow bigger, realizing their full potential in a rapidly changing marketplace.

TRACKING PROGRESS AND ADJUSTING GOALS

Tracking progress and adjusting goals is a critical component of the entrepreneurial journey. Small business owners must establish measurable objectives to gauge their growth and success. This involves developing success for their business, whether it's increasing revenue, expanding market reach, or enhancing customer satisfaction. By setting specific, attainable targets, entrepreneurs can create a roadmap that guides their efforts and enables them to celebrate milestones.

To effectively track progress, entrepreneurs should implement various measurement tools and techniques. Key performance indicators (KPIs) are essential for assessing growth in specific areas. These may include sales figures, customer acquisition costs, and overall pro stability. Project management software can also help track tasks and deadlines and ensure that business operations align with the established goals. Regularly reviewing these metrics allows business owners to identify trends, recognize achievements, and uncover areas needing improvement.

Adjusting goals in response to changing circumstances is equally essential for maintaining momentum. The business landscape is dynamic, and what might have been a relevant goal six months ago may no longer apply. Entrepreneurs should adopt a flexible mindset, allowing them to pivot when necessary. This could involve scaling back overly ambitious targets or setting more challenging goals in response to unexpected growth. Regularly revisiting goals ensures they remain aligned with both market conditions and the evolving vision of the business.

Feedback from customers, employees, and industry peers can provide invaluable insights into the effectiveness of current strategies. Conducting surveys, holding focus groups, and engaging in open conversations can show how well the business meets its objectives. This feedback loop not only aids in tracking progress but also informs necessary adjustments to goals. Entrepreneurs who remain receptive to external input are better positioned to adapt and thrive in a competitive environment.

Ultimately, tracking progress and adjusting goals is not merely a bureaucratic exercise but a vital practice fostering growth and innovation. By remaining vigilant and proactive, entrepreneurs can harness their insights to rethink their strategies, enhance their offerings, and nurture their entrepreneurial mindset. This commitment to continuous improvement positions their businesses for success and cultivates a culture of resilience and adaptability that is essential in today's fast-paced market.

Chapter 4: Embracing Risk and Uncertainty

UNDERSTANDING BUSINESS RISKS

Understanding business risks is essential for small business owners and entrepreneurs who aspire to grow and succeed in a competitive environment. Business risks can be de ned as the potential threats that may hinder an organization from achieving its objectives, impacting its profitability and longevity. Recognizing these risks is the first step toward effective management. Entrepreneurs must identify the risks, assess their potential impact, and develop mitigation strategies. By doing so, they can create a resilient business model adaptable to changes and challenges in the marketplace.

Entrepreneurs should consider various categories of business risks. Financial risks often arise from market conditions, interest rates, and credit availability fluctuations. Operational risks pertain to internal processes, systems, and human resources, which can affect the efficiency of operations. Compliance risks involve the possibility of legal penalties due to non-adherence with laws and regulations. Additionally, strategic risks can emerge from poor decision-making or failure to respond aptly to competitive pressures. Understanding these categories helps entrepreneurs pinpoint specific areas of vulnerability within their businesses.

Assessing business risks requires a systematic approach. Entrepreneurs should begin by conducting a thorough risk assessment that involves identifying potential challenges, analyzing their likelihood of occurrence, and evaluating their possible impact on the business. This process can include tools such as SWOT analysis, highlighting strengths, weaknesses, opportunities, and threats. By employing this analytical framework, business owners can prioritize risks based on severity and likelihood, allowing them to focus their resources on the most significant threats.

Once risks are identified and assessed, entrepreneurs must develop risk mitigation strategies tailored to their business context. This could involve implementing robust financial controls, diversifying product offerings, or investing in employee training to enhance operational efficiency. Creating a contingency plan for unexpected events can also provide a safety net that ensures business continuity. Engaging stakeholders, including employees and advisors, in the risk management process, fosters a culture of awareness and preparedness, allowing the organization to respond effectively to potential challenges.

Ultimately, understanding and managing business risks is a critical component of the entrepreneurial mindset. Entrepreneurs who actively engage in risk assessment and mitigation protect their businesses and position themselves for growth and innovation. By embracing a proactive approach to risk management, small business owners can build a sustainable enterprise that thrives even in uncertain conditions. This mindset enhances their decision-making capabilities and instills confidence among stakeholders, paving the way for long-term success in the competitive landscape.

DEVELOPING A RISK MANAGEMENT STRATEGY

Developing a risk management strategy is essential for small business owners and entrepreneurs who aspire to grow their ventures while navigating the market's uncertainties. The first step in this process involves identifying potential risks that could impact the business. These risks can be categorized into various types, including financial, operational, regulatory, and reputational risks. Conducting a thorough risk assessment allows entrepreneurs to pinpoint specific vulnerabilities within their operations and external environment. By understanding these risks, business owners can prioritize which ones to address based on their potential impact and likelihood of occurrence.

Once risks have been identified, the next phase is to evaluate their implications. This evaluation should consider the risk's severity and the business's capacity to absorb its potential consequences. Entrepreneurs should consider questions such as: What would happen if this risk materialized? How would it affect cash ow, customer relationships, or overall business sustainability? By analyzing these factors, business owners can develop a clearer picture of the risks they face and create a more tailored response strategy.

With a solid understanding of risks and their potential impacts, the next step is to develop specific mitigating strategies. Risk mitigation strategies can include transferring the risk through insurance, implementing operational controls to reduce the likelihood of occurrence, or developing contingency plans to respond effectively if a risk does materialize. It is essential to involve key stakeholders in this process, as they can provide valuable insights and contribute to a more comprehensive risk management approach. Engaging employees in discussions about risk can foster a culture of awareness and preparedness throughout the organization.

Monitoring and reviewing the risk management strategy is equally important. As the business environment evolves, so too will the risks that entrepreneurs face. Regularly revisiting the risk management strategy allows business owners to adjust their approaches based on new information, changing market conditions, or lessons learned from experiences. This iterative process ensures that the strategy remains relevant and practical, ultimately supporting the growth and resilience of the business.

Finally, communication of the risk management strategy is vital for its success. Small business owners should ensure that all employees understand the risks the business faces and their roles in managing those risks. Providing training and resources can empower employees to act proactively when risks arise. Furthermore, maintaining open lines of communication fosters an environment where team members feel comfortable reporting potential risks or concerns, leading to a more robust overall risk management culture. By embedding risk management into the organization's fabric, entrepreneurs can position their businesses for sustainable growth and long-term success.

BUILDING RESILIENCE IN THE FACE OF SETBACKS

Building resilience in the face of setbacks is critical to sustaining growth in any entrepreneurial journey. Setbacks are an inevitable part of running a business, whether in the form of financial losses, failed product launches, or unexpected changes in the market. Understanding how to develop resilience allows entrepreneurs to navigate these challenges effectively, turning obstacles into opportunities for learning and growth. This mindset helps business owners recover from difficulties and strengthens their ability to face future challenges with confidence.

One key aspect of building resilience is fostering a growth mindset. Entrepreneurs who adopt a growth mindset view challenges as learning opportunities rather than insurmountable barriers. This perspective encourages them to analyze setbacks critically, identifying the lessons that can be derived from each experience. For instance, if a marketing campaign fails to yield the expected results, instead of viewing it solely as a loss, an entrepreneur can examine the data to understand what went wrong and how similar mistakes can be avoided. This proactive approach to learning can significantly enhance an entrepreneur's adaptability and innovation.

Another vital element in cultivating resilience is the importance of a strong support network. Small business owners often face the burden of isolation, which can exacerbate feelings of defeat during tough times. By surrounding themselves with mentors, peers, and supportive friends or family, entrepreneurs can share their experiences and gain different perspectives on their challenges. Networking within industry groups and attending business workshops can provide valuable insights and encouragement. This sense of community offers emotional support and practical advice that can help navigate setbacks more effectively.

Additionally, developing coping strategies is essential for maintaining resilience. Entrepreneurs should create a toolkit of techniques they can employ when facing adversity. This may include stress management practices such as mindfulness meditation, exercise, or hobbies that provide a mental break from business pressures. Setting aside time for self-reflection can also be beneficial, allowing entrepreneurs to assess their emotional responses to setbacks and adjust their approaches accordingly. Business owners can enhance their capacity to bounce back from difficulties by prioritizing mental well-being.

Finally, entrepreneurs need to maintain a long-term perspective. Resilience is not solely about recovering from a single setback but about fostering a mindset that sees beyond immediate challenges to the broader vision of success. By developing a clear sense of purpose and goals, entrepreneurs can remind themselves of why they started their ventures in the first place. This clarity can motivate them to persevere through tough times, reinforcing their commitment to their business and its potential. In doing so, they cultivate personal resilience and a sustainable entrepreneurial spirit that drives continuous growth.

Chapter 5: Cultivating Creativity and Innovation

FOSTERING AN INNOVATIVE MINDSET

Fostering an innovative mindset is essential for small business owners and entrepreneurs who aspire to grow and thrive in a competitive landscape. A creative mindset is characterized by curiosity, a willingness to take risks, and an openness to learning from failures. Embracing these attributes can help entrepreneurs identify new opportunities, adapt to changing market conditions, and develop solutions that meet the evolving needs of their customers. It is essential to recognize that innovation is not just about creating groundbreaking products; it also encompasses improving processes, enhancing customer experiences, and finding new ways to deliver value.

To cultivate an innovative mindset, entrepreneurs should prioritize a culture of experimentation within their organizations. This involves encouraging team members to explore new ideas and take calculated risks without fearing punitive consequences for failure. By promoting an environment where experimentation is valued, businesses can unlock creativity and empower employees to contribute to problem-solving initiatives. This approach leads to innovative solutions and fosters a sense of ownership and engagement among team members, which is crucial for long-term success.

Another critical aspect of fostering an innovative mindset is continuous learning. Entrepreneurs should actively seek out personal and professional development opportunities through workshops, seminars, or networking events. Engaging with peers and industry leaders can inspire new ideas and provide fresh perspectives on existing challenges. Additionally, staying informed about industry trends and emerging technologies can help entrepreneurs anticipate shifts in the market and position their businesses accordingly. By committing to lifelong learning, entrepreneurs can cultivate a mindset that embraces change and adapts quickly.

Collaboration is also a key factor in fostering innovation. Entrepreneurs can benefit from forming partnerships with other businesses, academic institutions, and community organizations. These collaborations can lead to exchanging ideas, resources, and expertise that drive innovation. By leveraging the strengths of various stakeholders, small business owners can create a more dynamic and resourceful environment that encourages creative problem-solving. This collaborative spirit accelerates innovation and strengthens the business's network, opening up new avenues for growth.

Finally, embracing a customer-centric approach is vital for fostering an innovative mindset. Entrepreneurs should actively seek customer feedback and incorporate their insights into product development and service enhancements. Understanding the needs and preferences of the target audience allows for more tailored solutions and can spark innovative ideas that resonate with customers. By placing the customer at the center of their innovation efforts, small business owners can ensure that their initiatives drive growth and enhance customer satisfaction and loyalty, ultimately leading to sustainable success in the marketplace.

TECHNIQUES FOR ENHANCING CREATIVITY

Creativity is crucial for small business owners and entrepreneurs looking to differentiate themselves in a competitive marketplace. Enhancing creativity can lead to innovative products, unique marketing strategies, and more efficient processes. One effective technique for stimulating creativity is brainstorming. This involves generating a large number of ideas in a short period without judgment or criticism. Entrepreneurs can tap into diverse perspectives by creating an open environment where all ideas are welcome, fostering a collaborative culture that encourages risk-taking and experimentation.

Another valuable technique is the practice of mind mapping. This visual tool helps entrepreneurs organize their thoughts and explore connections between ideas. By placing a central concept in the middle and branching out into related topics, business owners can visualize their ideas in a structured yet flexible manner. This technique not only aids in clarity but also promotes the discovery of new avenues for innovation. Mind mapping can be particularly beneficial during the planning phases of a new project or when seeking solutions to complex problems, allowing entrepreneurs to see the bigger picture.

Setting aside dedicated time for creative thinking is also essential. Finding time for reflection and idea generation can be challenging in the hustle and bustle of running a business. However, carving out specific periods in the schedule for creative thinking can lead to significant breakthroughs. This could involve engaging in activities that inspire creativity, such as taking walks, reading, or even meditating. By prioritizing creative time, entrepreneurs can refresh their minds, making space for new ideas to emerge and allowing them to approach challenges with renewed energy.

Collaboration with others can further enhance creativity. Engaging with individuals from diverse backgrounds or industries can spark new ideas and perspectives. Networking events, workshops, and informal peer discussions can inspire fresh insights. This exchange of ideas can lead to innovative solutions that entrepreneurs may not have considered. By fostering a culture of collaboration, small business owners can build a support network that encourages creative thinking and collective problem-solving.

Lastly, embracing failure as a part of the creative process is vital for growth. Many entrepreneurs fear making mistakes, which can stifle their creativity. However, understanding that failure is often a stepping stone to success can liberate entrepreneurs from the fear of taking risks. Business owners can cultivate a mindset that embraces experimentation and innovation by viewing failures as learning opportunities. This shift in perspective enhances individual creativity and contributes to a resilient, adaptable business culture in the face of challenges.

IMPLEMENTING INNOVATIVE IDEAS

Implementing innovative ideas is critical to fostering growth within any small business. Small business owners and entrepreneurs must recognize that creativity is not solely the domain of large corporations. The agility and flexibility inherent in smaller enterprises provide a unique advantage. This advantage can be harnessed to explore new ideas, adapt to market changes, and differentiate from competitors. Entrepreneurs can position their businesses for success in an ever-evolving marketplace by cultivating an environment that encourages innovation.

Adopting a structured approach is essential to implement innovative ideas effectively. This begins with identifying areas within the business that could benefit from innovation. Entrepreneurs should thoroughly analyze their operations, customer feedback, and industry trends. This assessment will help pinpoint where improvements can be made or where new opportunities exist. Once these areas are identified, entrepreneurs can brainstorm potential solutions and innovations, ensuring the ideas align with the business's vision and the target audience's needs.

Collaboration plays a vital role in the implementation of innovative ideas. Small business owners should foster a culture that encourages input from all team members. Diverse perspectives can lead to more creative solutions and enhance decision-making. Entrepreneurs tap into a wealth of ideas by involving employees in the innovation process and increasing employee engagement and investment in the outcome. Regular brainstorming sessions, idea-sharing platforms, and collaborative projects facilitate this culture of innovation, making every team member feel valued and empowered.

Once potential innovations are identified and developed, the next step is to create an implementation plan. This plan should outline the necessary resources, timelines, and key performance indicators to measure success. Entrepreneurs must also consider potential risks and develop strategies to mitigate them. Involving stakeholders in this planning phase can provide additional insights and foster a sense of ownership over the innovation process. Clear communication and alignment of goals are essential to ensure that everyone is on board and understands their role in bringing innovative ideas to life.

Finally, entrepreneurs must remain adaptable after implementing innovative ideas. The business landscape is dynamic, and what works today may not be effective tomorrow. Continuous evaluation of the implemented innovations is necessary to assess their impact and adjust as needed. Encouraging feedback from customers and employees will provide valuable insights into the effectiveness of the changes. By embracing a mindset of ongoing improvement, small business owners can sustain their competitive edge and drive long-term growth, transforming innovative ideas into lasting success.

Chapter 6: Building a Strong Support Network

THE ROLE OF MENTORSHIP IN GROWTH

Mentorship plays a pivotal role in the growth of small business owners and entrepreneurs. As individuals embark on their entrepreneurial journeys, their challenges often seem insurmountable. A mentor provides invaluable guidance, sharing their experiences and insights, which can help navigate the complexities of business ownership. Mentors empower entrepreneurs to make informed decisions and avoid common pitfalls by fostering a relationship built on trust and mutual respect. This support system enables entrepreneurs to think critically about their strategies and to approach problems with a more seasoned perspective.

One of the primary benefits of mentorship is the transfer of knowledge. Experienced mentors often possess industry-specific knowledge and practical skills that can significantly enhance an entrepreneur's capabilities. They can provide guidance on essential aspects of running a business, such as financial management, marketing strategies, and operational efficiency. This knowledge transfer shortens the learning curve for new entrepreneurs and equips them with tools and techniques that can be critical for their business growth. Furthermore, mentors can introduce their mentees to valuable resources and networks, creating opportunities that may otherwise be inaccessible.

Mentorship also encourages self-reflection and personal development. Engaging with a mentor often prompts entrepreneurs to step back and evaluate their goals, values, and strategies. This process of introspection can lead to a deeper understanding of their strengths and weaknesses, fostering a growth mindset. Mentors challenge their mentees to think bigger, pushing them to step outside their comfort zones, explore innovative ideas, and embrace calculated risks. This encouragement is essential for cultivating resilience and adaptability, which are crucial for success in the ever-evolving business landscape.

Moreover, the emotional support provided by mentors cannot be overstated. Entrepreneurship can be a lonely journey filled with highs and lows. A mentor serves not only as an advisor but also as a sounding board during challenging times. They can offer reassurance and encouragement, boosting an entrepreneur's confidence and motivation. This emotional connection helps to alleviate feelings of isolation and provides a sense of community, reminding entrepreneurs that they are not alone in their struggles. This support is vital for maintaining mental well-being and sustaining long-term commitment to their business goals.

In conclusion, the role of mentorship in the growth of small business owners and entrepreneurs is multifaceted and profound. Mentors play an essential part in shaping the entrepreneurial mindset needed for success by providing knowledge, encouraging self-reflection, and offering emotional support. Entrepreneurs who actively seek out and cultivate mentorship relationships are better positioned to navigate the complexities of their business journeys. As they embrace mentorship, they enhance their growth and contribute to a culture of support and collaboration within the entrepreneurial community, ultimately fostering a more robust ecosystem for innovation and success.

NETWORKING STRATEGIES FOR ENTREPRENEURS

Networking is a fundamental pillar for entrepreneurs seeking to expand their businesses and enhance their growth trajectory. Connecting with the right people can open doors to new opportunities, partnerships, and resources crucial for success. Entrepreneurs should actively engage in networking activities that align with their business goals and personal growth. This includes attending industry conferences, participating in local business groups, and leveraging social media platforms to foster connections with like-minded individuals.

One effective networking strategy is to prioritize quality over quantity. Instead of attempting to meet as many people as possible, entrepreneurs should focus on building meaningful relationships with a select group of individuals who can provide value. This involves understanding their needs and challenges and offering assistance or insights that can benefit them. By nurturing these relationships, entrepreneurs can create a supportive network that contributes to their professional development and business success.

Additionally, entrepreneurs should embrace the concept of collaboration over competition. Networking should not be viewed as a zero-sum game; instead, it is an opportunity to build alliances with others in the industry. Businesses can share resources, knowledge, and expertise by collaborating with fellow entrepreneurs. Such partnerships can lead to innovative solutions and new ideas, ultimately driving growth for all parties involved. Entrepreneurs need to approach networking with a mindset of abundance, recognizing that shared success can elevate the entire community.

Another critical aspect of effective networking is the art of follow-up. After initial meetings or introductions, entrepreneurs must take the initiative to maintain contact with their new connections. This can be achieved through personalized emails, social media interactions, or even scheduling coffee meetings. Consistent follow-up reinforces the relationship and keeps the entrepreneur's business top-of-mind. In these ongoing conversations, deeper connections are formed, leading to potential collaborations or referrals.

Finally, entrepreneurs should always be prepared to share their stories and insights during networking. A compelling personal narrative can captivate an audience and make connections more memorable. By articulating their vision, values, and the unique aspects of their business, entrepreneurs can engage others and inspire interest in what they do. This storytelling approach humanizes the entrepreneur and fosters authenticity, making it easier for others to relate and connect personally. Through these strategic networking practices, entrepreneurs can cultivate a robust network that supports their growth ambitions.

COLLABORATING WITH PEERS AND PARTNERS

Collaborating with peers and partners is vital to fostering an entrepreneurial mindset geared toward growth. Building relationships with like-minded individuals and organizations can amplify your resources, knowledge, and opportunities. Small business owners can leverage diverse perspectives and skills through collaborative efforts, allowing innovative solutions and improved problem-solving capabilities. This chapter underscores the significance of collaboration and offers practical insights into establishing and nurturing these relationships for mutual growth.

One of the primary benefits of collaboration is the ability to share resources. When entrepreneurs partner with others, they can pool their financial, intellectual, or technological assets, creating a more robust foundation for success. For instance, small business owners can share marketing platforms, co-develop products, or even engage in joint ventures. Such arrangements can significantly reduce costs and risks associated with entrepreneurship. Identifying the right partners who align with your business values and goals is essential for maximizing these advantages.

Knowledge sharing is another critical aspect of collaboration. Engaging with peers with different experiences or expertise can provide invaluable insights that inform decision-making. For example, entrepreneurs can participate in workshops, networking events, or online forums to exchange ideas and best practices. This collaborative learning environment encourages adaptation and innovation, which are crucial for sustained growth. By actively seeking mentors and peers who challenge your thinking and offer constructive feedback, you can enhance your entrepreneurial skills and broaden your perspective.

Building a solid network of collaborators also fosters accountability. When you surround yourself with motivated individuals who share your ambitions, you create a support system that encourages you to stay focused and committed to your goals. Regular check-ins with partners can help you track progress, celebrate successes, and address challenges collectively. This shared sense of responsibility can drive you to push beyond your limits, ultimately leading to more significant achievements. Establishing a culture of accountability within your collaborations can significantly impact your business trajectory.

Finally, successful collaboration requires effective communication and trust. Open dialogue is essential for understanding each party's expectations, strengths, and weaknesses. Establishing clear goals and roles can prevent misunderstandings and foster a more productive partnership. Nurturing trust through transparency and reliability will also encourage a positive collaborative environment. As you cultivate these relationships, remember that collaboration is a two-way street; being willing to give as much as you receive will lead to more fruitful and enduring partnerships. Embracing collaboration enhances your entrepreneurial mindset and positions your business for scalable growth in an increasingly interconnected world.

Chapter 7: Learning from Failure

ANALYZING FAILURES FOR GROWTH

Analyzing failures is a crucial aspect of the entrepreneurial journey that can lead to significant growth and development. Understanding why a venture or strategy did not succeed is essential for small business owners and entrepreneurs. This process involves a deep dive into the failure's circumstances, identifying contributing factors, and extracting valuable lessons. By adopting a mindset that views failure as a learning opportunity rather than a setback, entrepreneurs can transform negative experiences into stepping stones for future success.

One of the first steps in analyzing failures is to conduct a thorough debriefing. This involves gathering the team involved in the project and discussing what went wrong. Encouraging open and honest dialogue can help uncover insights that might not be immediately apparent. It is essential to create an environment where team members feel safe to express their thoughts without fear of judgment. During this process, entrepreneurs should focus on the facts rather than emotions, distinguishing between external market factors and internal decisions that may have led to the failure.

After identifying the contributing factors, the next step is categorizing these insights into actionable lessons. This might include recognizing patterns in decision-making, understanding customer feedback, or evaluating market conditions. Entrepreneurs can create a reference guide for future projects by documenting these lessons. This systematic approach enhances individual learning and fosters a culture of continuous improvement within the organization. Embracing this culture encourages team members to take calculated risks, knowing that failures can lead to valuable insights.

Moreover, analyzing failures can reveal areas for personal and professional growth. Entrepreneurs often wear multiple hats, and understanding where their skills may have fallen short can highlight development opportunities. This might mean seeking additional training, mentorship, or collaborating with others with complementary skills. By acknowledging their limitations, entrepreneurs can cultivate a growth mindset that propels them toward more informed decision-making.

Lastly, sharing the insights from failure with the broader entrepreneurial community is vital. Whether through networking events, social media, or industry publications, discussing failures and the lessons learned can inspire others. This transparency enhances credibility and fosters a supportive environment where all entrepreneurs can learn from each other's experiences. Ultimately, by analyzing failures effectively and embracing the lessons they offer, small business owners can position themselves for sustained growth and success in a competitive landscape.

CASE STUDIES OF SUCCESSFUL ENTREPRENEURS

In entrepreneurship, real-life success stories are powerful illustrations of the principles underpinning a growth-oriented mindset. Analyzing the journeys of successful entrepreneurs provides valuable insights into the strategies, challenges, and mentalities that foster significant business expansion. This subchapter delves into various case studies that exemplify how specific approaches to challenges can lead to remarkable achievements, offering inspiration and practical lessons for small business owners.

One prominent example is Howard Schultz, the former CEO of Starbucks. Schultz transformed a small coffee shop chain into a global phenomenon by recognizing the importance of creating an experience rather than merely selling coffee. His entrepreneurial vision focused on building a community around the brand, emphasizing customer experience and employee satisfaction. Schultz's journey highlights the significance of understanding market needs and leveraging them to cultivate a loyal customer base, underscoring the necessity of adaptability and innovation in sustaining growth.

Another instructive case is Sara Blakely, the founder of Spanx. Blakely's story is a testament to the power of resilience and creativity in overcoming obstacles. With only $5,000 in savings and no formal business training, she identified a gap in the market for comfortable yet stylish undergarments. Blakely's ability to embrace failure and learn from her experiences allowed her to innovate continuously. Her journey emphasizes the importance of self-belief and the willingness to take calculated risks, providing a roadmap for aspiring entrepreneurs seeking to carve their paths in competitive industries.

Elon Musk, the founder of companies like Tesla and SpaceX, exemplifies the entrepreneurial mindset characterized by relentless ambition and visionary thinking. Musk's ventures often challenge the status quo, driven by a desire to solve significant global issues, such as sustainable energy and space exploration. His case illustrates how setting audacious goals can inspire personal growth and drive entire industries forward. Small business owners can learn from Musk's approach to fostering a culture of innovation, encouraging their teams to think beyond conventional boundaries and pursue transformative ideas.

Lastly, the story of Oprah Winfrey demonstrates the profound impact of personal branding and authenticity in business. Rising from humble beginnings, Winfrey built a media empire centered around her genuine connection with her audience. She created a brand synonymous with empowerment and inspiration by leveraging her unique narrative and values. Winfrey's success highlights the importance of authenticity in entrepreneurship; small business owners should embrace their unique stories and values as powerful tools for differentiation in the marketplace, fostering deeper connections with their customers and enhancing brand loyalty.

These case studies illustrate that successful entrepreneurs share resilience, adaptability, and a willingness to innovate. By studying their journeys, small business owners can glean insights into the entrepreneurial mindset necessary for growth. Embracing these principles can empower them to navigate their unique challenges, leading to sustained success and realizing their ambitious visions.

TURNING SETBACKS INTO OPPORTUNITIES

Setbacks are an inevitable part of the entrepreneurial journey, and how one responds to these challenges often determines future success. Viewing setbacks purely as failures can lead to a negative spiral, stifling creativity and growth. Instead, shifting the focus towards turning these setbacks into opportunities can foster resilience and innovation. Small business owners and entrepreneurs can cultivate an entrepreneurial mindset that embraces challenges as crucial learning experiences, propelling them toward more significant achievements.

One effective strategy for turning setbacks into opportunities is to conduct a thorough analysis of what went wrong. This involves reflecting on decisions, actions, and external factors contributing to the setback. By pinpointing the root causes, entrepreneurs can gain valuable insights that inform future strategies. This analytical approach helps prevent similar issues and opens up avenues for innovative solutions that may not have been considered previously. Learning from mistakes is a hallmark of successful entrepreneurs, and this willingness to dissect setbacks fosters growth.

Networking and collaboration can serve as powerful tools in transforming setbacks into opportunities. Building a robust support system of fellow entrepreneurs, mentors, and industry professionals can provide diverse perspectives and advice during challenging times. Engaging with others allows for the sharing of experiences, which can illuminate paths forward that may not have been apparent. Additionally, collaboration can lead to co-creating solutions or partnerships that enhance business resilience. Entrepreneurs can leverage collective wisdom to navigate setbacks more effectively by seeking input from a broad network.

Adopting a growth mindset is essential in the face of setbacks. This mindset encourages individuals to view challenges as personal and professional development opportunities. Small business owners can train themselves to embrace discomfort and uncertainty, recognizing that these feelings often accompany significant growth. By reframing setbacks as integral components of their entrepreneurial journey, business owners can foster a more positive outlook that encourages perseverance. This shift cultivates an environment where innovation thrives, as risks are seen not as threats but as potential gateways to new ideas and ventures.

Finally, setting clear, flexible goals can aid in navigating setbacks and turning them into opportunities. Goals should not only focus on outcomes but also on the processes that lead to success. By establishing adaptable goals, entrepreneurs can adjust their strategies in response to setbacks without losing sight of their ultimate vision. This flexibility allows for real-time course corrections and encourages an ongoing commitment to learning and improvement. As small business owners embrace this dynamic approach, they will know that setbacks can often serve as catalysts for unexpected growth and success, reinforcing that resilience is a key component of the entrepreneurial mindset.

Chapter 8: Continuous Learning and Adaptation

EMBRACING LIFELONG LEARNING

Embracing lifelong learning is a fundamental concept that every small business owner and entrepreneur should integrate into their operational philosophy. The business landscape constantly evolves, influenced by technological advancements, market shifts, and consumer behavior changes. Entrepreneurs must adopt a mindset prioritizing continuous education and skill development to thrive in this dynamic environment. This approach enhances personal growth and drives business innovation and competitiveness.

One of the key aspects of lifelong learning is the recognition that knowledge acquisition does not cease after formal education. Entrepreneurs should actively seek opportunities to expand their understanding through various channels, such as workshops, online courses, industry conferences, and networking events. These platforms provide invaluable insights into emerging trends, best practices, and innovative strategies to implement within one's business. By remaining engaged and curious, entrepreneurs position themselves to adapt quickly to new challenges and seize opportunities as they arise.

Moreover, embracing lifelong learning encourages a culture of adaptability, which is crucial for long-term success. In a world where change is the only constant, being open to new ideas and perspectives can differentiate successful entrepreneurs from those who become stagnant. This adaptability applies to personal skill sets and extends to business models and operational practices. By fostering a learning environment within their organizations, entrepreneurs empower their teams to explore new ideas, experiment with solutions, and ultimately drive the business forward.

Another sign that can't be of lifelong learning is the enhancement of problem-solving capabilities. Entrepreneurs often face complex challenges that require innovative solutions. By continuously acquiring knowledge and skills, they develop a broader toolkit to tackle these obstacles effectively. Engaging with diverse learning materials and experiences allows entrepreneurs to draw connections between seemingly unrelated concepts, fostering creativity and critical thinking. This ability to think outside the box can lead to breakthrough innovations and improved business processes.

Lastly, lifelong learning is not just about individual growth; it also strengthens relationships within the entrepreneurial community. By participating in learning opportunities, entrepreneurs can connect with peers, mentors, and industry leaders who share their passion for growth. These relationships can lead to collaborations, partnerships, and support networks that are invaluable in navigating the entrepreneurial journey. As small business owners and entrepreneurs embrace lifelong learning, they enhance their potential and contribute to a vibrant ecosystem that fosters innovation and progress.

STAYING INFORMED ABOUT INDUSTRY TRENDS

Staying informed about industry trends is essential for small business owners and entrepreneurs who aspire to grow and innovate. The business landscape constantly evolves, influenced by technological advancements, shifting consumer behaviors, and emerging competition.

To remain relevant and competitive, entrepreneurs must cultivate a habit of continuous learning and engagement with the broader industry landscape. This proactive approach helps identify new opportunities and understand potential challenges that could impact the business.

One effective way to keep abreast of industry trends is to establish a routine of consuming relevant content. Subscribing to industry-specific publications, newsletters, and blogs can provide valuable insights into market dynamics. Podcasts and webinars also serve as excellent resources for gaining knowledge from thought leaders and experts in the field. By dedicating time each week to consume this information, entrepreneurs can better anticipate shifts in their industry and adapt their strategies accordingly. Staying informed empowers business owners to make data-driven decisions that align with current market conditions.

Networking plays a crucial role in staying informed as well. Engaging with peers, mentors, and industry experts can provide firsthand knowledge of emerging trends and best practices. Attending industry conferences, workshops, and local business events offers opportunities to exchange ideas and experiences with others facing similar challenges. These interactions can lead to valuable collaborations and partnerships, further enhancing a business's ability to adapt and grow. The connections made through networking can also serve as a sounding board for new ideas, helping entrepreneurs refine their strategies based on shared experiences.

Social media platforms and professional networks can also enhance an entrepreneur's understanding of industry trends. Following industry leaders, influencers, and relevant organizations on platforms like LinkedIn and Twitter can provide real-time updates and insights. Engaging in discussions and sharing content can help entrepreneurs stay informed and position themselves as thought leaders within their networks. This visibility can attract new opportunities and foster relationships, contributing to business growth.

Entrepreneurs should consider implementing a systematic approach to trend analysis. This can involve regularly reviewing key performance indicators (KPIs) and market research data to identify patterns and shifts in consumer behavior. Creating a trend report can help consolidate findings and facilitate strategic planning sessions. By fostering a culture of curiosity and adaptation within their organizations, small business owners can remain agile and responsive to the ever-changing business environment. Embracing industry trends as a vital component of their growth strategy will equip entrepreneurs with the insights to scale their businesses effectively.

ADAPTING TO CHANGE EFFECTIVELY

In the ever-evolving business landscape, adapting to change effectively is not just a skill but an essential mindset for small business owners and entrepreneurs. The ability to pivot in response to market shifts, technological advancements, or consumer preferences can distinguish thriving enterprises from those that struggle to survive. Embracing change requires a proactive approach that encourages flexibility and innovation. This adaptability is rooted in a deep understanding of both internal capabilities and external conditions.

To adapt successfully, entrepreneurs must cultivate a curiosity and openness mindset. This involves seeking information about industry trends, customer feedback, and competitor strategies. Small business owners can identify opportunities and threats that require attention by remaining engaged with the broader business environment. Engaging in continuous learning through workshops, networking events, and online courses can enhance this knowledge base, equipping entrepreneurs with the insights necessary to make informed decisions.

Moreover, fostering a culture of adaptability within a business is crucial. This means encouraging team members to share ideas, voice concerns, and propose innovative solutions. Employees who feel empowered to contribute are more likely to embrace changes and support the organization's goals. Implementing regular brainstorming sessions and feedback loops can create a dynamic workplace where adaptability is part of the organizational DNA. Recognizing and rewarding flexibility and creative problem-solving can motivate employees to engage positively with change.

Another key aspect of adapting to change effectively is leveraging technology. In today's digital age, technological tools can streamline operations, enhance customer engagement, and provide valuable data analytics. Small business owners should invest in technology that aligns with their strategic objectives and enables them to respond to changes swiftly. For example, utilizing customer relationship management (CRM) systems can help businesses better understand customers' needs and preferences, allowing for timely adjustments in offerings and marketing strategies.

Resilience plays a pivotal role in navigating change. Entrepreneurs need to recognize that not every change will lead to immediate success. Challenges and setbacks are part of the entrepreneurial journey. Developing resilience involves maintaining a positive outlook and learning from failures. By framing obstacles as opportunities for growth, small business owners can foster a mindset that not only adapts to change but thrives in it, ultimately positioning their businesses for sustainable development in an unpredictable world.

Chapter 9: Developing Leadership Skills

THE IMPORTANCE OF LEADERSHIP IN BUSINESS

Leadership plays a pivotal role in the success of any business, particularly for small business owners and entrepreneurs. Effective leadership not only influences the internal dynamics of a team but also shapes the external perception of the company. Leaders set the vision and direction, ensuring everyone is aligned toward common goals. In a competitive market, the ability of a leader to inspire and motivate employees can significantly impact productivity and employee retention, which are crucial for the sustainability of small enterprises. By fostering a strong organizational culture, leaders can cultivate an environment where innovation thrives, leading to growth and adaptability.

Moreover, leadership is essential in navigating the challenges that small businesses face. Entrepreneurs often encounter unforeseen obstacles, from financial constraints to market fluctuations. A strong leader demonstrates resilience and adaptability, guiding their team through uncertainty. By maintaining open lines of communication and encouraging feedback, leaders can create a safe space for employees to express concerns and ideas. This collaborative approach helps in problem-solving and builds trust within the team, making it easier to overcome challenges together.

In addition to internal management, effective leadership enhances customer relationships. Leaders who prioritize customer satisfaction and instill this value within their teams can significantly improve service quality. When employees feel empowered and supported by their leaders, they are likelier to go the extra mile for customers, enhancing brand loyalty. A leader's commitment to understanding customer needs and responding to feedback establishes a customer-centric culture that can differentiate a business in a crowded marketplace.

Furthermore, leadership is integral to strategic decision-making. Small business owners must be agile and innovative to grow their enterprises consistently. Leaders who adopt a growth-oriented mindset are more inclined to seek new opportunities, whether through expanding product lines, entering new markets, or leveraging technology. By encouraging continuous learning and experimentation, leaders can position their businesses to seize emerging trends and adapt to changing consumer preferences, ultimately driving long-term success.

Lastly, the importance of leadership extends beyond the confines of the organization. Leaders serve as role models within their communities in influencing the entrepreneurial landscape. Small business leaders can inspire other entrepreneurs by demonstrating ethical practices, social responsibility, and a commitment to diversity and inclusion, as well as by contributing positively to the local economy. This ripple effect of strong leadership fosters a supportive entrepreneurial ecosystem and encourages collaboration and partnership among businesses, amplifying growth opportunities for all.

KEY LEADERSHIP TRAITS FOR ENTREPRENEURS

Leadership is a crucial component of entrepreneurial success, as it directly influences a business's growth trajectory and ability to navigate challenges. Entrepreneurs must cultivate traits that foster resilience and inspire their teams and stakeholders. Among these traits, vision, adaptability, decisiveness, emotional intelligence, and integrity stand out as foundational elements that entrepreneurs should prioritize in their personal and professional development.

Vision is the cornerstone of effective leadership. Entrepreneurs with a clear and compelling vision can articulate their goals and inspire others to work toward a shared future. This trait enables leaders to set strategic directions and motivate their teams to embrace the growth journey. A well-de ned vision is a guiding star, helping entrepreneurs make informed decisions and prioritize initiatives that align with their long-term objectives. Leaders can create a unified and purpose-driven organizational culture by consistently communicating this vision.

Adaptability is another essential trait for entrepreneurs, particularly in today's fast-paced business environment. The ability to pivot in response to market changes, consumer preferences, or unforeseen challenges is vital for long-term survival and growth. Entrepreneurs who demonstrate adaptability are likelier to embrace innovation and encourage their teams to explore creative solutions. This flexibility helps businesses stay relevant and fosters a culture of continuous improvement, where learning from failure is viewed as a stepping stone to success.

Decisiveness is critical for entrepreneurs, who often face complex decisions with limited information. The capacity to make timely and informed choices can differentiate successful leaders from those who struggle to move their businesses forward. Decisive leaders instill confidence in their teams as they commit to action and accountability. This trait encourages a proactive approach to problem-solving and reinforces the notion that calculated risks are an inherent part of the entrepreneurial journey.

Emotional intelligence is increasingly recognized as a pivotal leadership trait. Entrepreneurs with high emotional intelligence can navigate interpersonal relationships with empathy and understanding. This ability to connect with others enhances collaboration and fosters a supportive work environment where team members feel valued and motivated. By leveraging emotional intelligence, entrepreneurs can better manage stress, resolve conflicts, and cultivate a culture of open communication, which is essential for sustaining growth and innovation.

Integrity is the key trait that underpins effective leadership. Entrepreneurs who lead with integrity build trust among their employees, customers, and business partners. This trust is essential for creating a positive reputation and fostering loyalty, which is vital for long-term success. Integrity involves being transparent, accountable, and ethical in business practices, ensuring that decisions reflect the values and mission of the organization. By embodying integrity, entrepreneurs enhance their credibility and set a powerful example for their teams, ultimately contributing to a sustainable and growth-oriented business culture.

BUILDING AND LEADING A HIGH-PERFORMING TEAM

Building and leading a high-performing team is essential for small business owners and entrepreneurs who aspire to scale their operations and achieve sustainable growth. A high-performing team is characterized by its ability to collaborate effectively, innovate consistently, and drive results that align with the organization's goals. To cultivate such a team, leaders must begin by identifying and assembling individuals whose skills, experiences, and values complement one another. This diversity enhances creativity and problem-solving and fosters an environment where team members can learn from each other and challenge one another to reach greater heights.

Effective communication is the cornerstone of any high-performing team. Entrepreneurs must establish open lines of communication to ensure that team members feel comfortable sharing ideas, feedback, and concerns. Regular team meetings, one-on-one check-ins, and collaborative tools can facilitate this communication. Additionally, leaders should model transparency by sharing the company's vision, goals, and challenges with their teams. When team members understand the bigger picture, they are more likely to feel a sense of ownership over their roles and contribute meaningfully to the team's success.

Empowering team members is another critical aspect of building a high-performing team. Small business owners should delegate responsibilities and trust their employees to execute tasks effectively. Empowerment involves providing the necessary resources, training, and support to help team members excel. Leaders should encourage autonomy by allowing individuals to make decisions within their areas of expertise, fostering a sense of accountability and pride in their work. This not only boosts morale but also enhances the team's overall productivity.

Recognition and feedback play significant roles in maintaining high performance within a team. Regularly acknowledging individual and team achievements reinforces positive behaviors and motivates members to strive for excellence. Constructive feedback should be provided promptly, focusing on specific behaviors and outcomes rather than personal attributes. This approach helps team members understand areas for improvement while feeling valued and supported in their growth journey.

Fostering a continuous learning and adaptation culture is vital for sustaining high performance. Entrepreneurs should encourage their teams to pursue professional development opportunities, attend workshops, and engage in knowledge-sharing sessions. This commitment to growth equips team members with new skills and instills a mindset of resilience and innovation. As the business landscape evolves, a high-performing team that embraces change and seeks improvement will be better positioned to navigate challenges and seize new growth opportunities.

Chapter 10: Scaling Your Business

IDENTIFYING GROWTH OPPORTUNITIES

Identifying growth opportunities is a vital aspect of nurturing a thriving business. For small business owners and entrepreneurs, the ability to pinpoint and capitalize on these opportunities can catalyze expansion and increase profitability. The entrepreneurial mindset hinges on a keen awareness of the market landscape, competitive dynamics, and emerging trends. By cultivating a habit of continuous observation and analysis, entrepreneurs can better position themselves to recognize potential avenues for growth that align with their vision and capabilities.

One of the primary methods for identifying growth opportunities is conducting thorough market research. This involves gathering data on customer preferences, industry trends, and competitor performance. Entrepreneurs should utilize quantitative and qualitative research methods, such as surveys, interviews, and sales data analysis, to paint a comprehensive market picture. Understanding the nuances of consumer behavior and the competitive landscape can reveal gaps your business can fill, whether through innovative products, improved services, or enhanced customer experiences.

Another approach to uncovering growth opportunities is to leverage the power of networking. Engaging with other entrepreneurs, industry experts, and potential customers can provide insights that may not be readily available through traditional research methods. Networking allows for exchanging ideas, experiences, and best practices that can spark new concepts for growth. Entrepreneurs can build relationships that lead to collaborative ventures or new market insights by participating in local business events, industry conferences, and online forums.

Furthermore, adopting a mindset of innovation is crucial for recognizing and seizing growth opportunities. Entrepreneurs must embrace a culture of creativity within their organizations, encouraging team members to think outside the box and propose new ideas. This can be achieved through brainstorming sessions, innovation workshops, and fostering an environment where experimentation is welcomed. By prioritizing innovation, businesses can stay ahead of the curve and adapt to changes in the market, ultimately leading to new product lines, services, or even entirely new business models.

Lastly, entrepreneurs must regularly assess their strengths and weaknesses regarding growth opportunities. A SWOT analysis can clarify internal capabilities and external market conditions. By understanding where their business excels and where improvements are needed, entrepreneurs can make informed decisions about which growth opportunities to pursue. This self-awareness not only aids in strategic planning but also empowers entrepreneurs to allocate resources effectively, ensuring that they are ready to capitalize on the most promising growth opportunities.

STRATEGIES FOR SCALING OPERATIONS

Scaling operations effectively requires a strategic approach that aligns with your business goals and market dynamics. The first step in this journey is to assess your current operational capabilities. This involves a thorough evaluation of your resources, processes, and workforce. Entrepreneurs must identify areas that are ripe for improvement and those that are already performing well. By understanding the strengths and weaknesses of your operations, you can prioritize which aspects to enhance first. This assessment can also reveal potential bottlenecks hindering growth if not addressed early.

Once you have a clear picture of your operational landscape, the following strategy involves leveraging technology to streamline processes. Automation tools and software solutions can significantly enhance productivity by reducing manual tasks and minimizing errors. For instance, customer relationship management (CRM) systems can improve client interactions, while inventory management software can optimize stock levels. Investing in technology increases efficiency and frees up valuable time for your team to focus on strategic initiatives that drive growth. Embracing digital transformation is no longer optional; it is essential for scaling effectively in today's competitive environment.

Another crucial strategy is to build a scalable organizational structure. As your business grows, the complexity of operations often increases, necessitating a clear hierarchy and defined roles. Developing a structure that allows for delegation and empowers employees is vital. This means creating teams that can operate independently while aligning with the company's vision. Regular training and development programs equip your staff with the necessary skills to meet new challenges. By fostering a culture of ownership and accountability, you enable your team to contribute actively to the scaling process.

Additionally, forging strategic partnerships can play a pivotal role in scaling operations. Collaborating with other businesses can provide access to new markets, resources, and expertise that would be challenging to achieve independently. These partnerships can take various forms, such as joint ventures, alliances, or even outsourcing certain functions. By pooling resources and sharing risks, you can enhance your capacity to scale without overextending your internal capabilities. Choosing partners whose values and objectives align with your own is essential to ensure a mutually beneficial relationship.

Finally, focusing on customer feedback and market trends is indispensable for sustainable growth. As you scale, keeping a pulse on customer needs and preferences is essential. Implementing feedback loops through surveys, social media, or direct interactions can provide valuable insights that inform your operational strategies. Being agile and responsive to market changes will allow your business to adapt quickly, ensuring that your scaling efforts resonate with your target audience. A customer-centric approach will ultimately drive growth and foster loyalty, setting the foundation for long-term success.

MANAGING GROWTH SUSTAINABLY

Managing growth sustainably is a critical aspect of entrepreneurship that ensures long-term success without compromising the integrity of the business. For small business owners and entrepreneurs, understanding how to balance expansion with sustainability can significantly impact their operational effectiveness and brand reputation. Sustainable growth involves increasing revenues and maintaining the quality of products or services, fostering a positive company culture, and being mindful of business activities' environmental and social impacts.

The first step in sustainably managing growth is developing a clear strategic plan. This plan should include realistic goals, timelines, and metrics for success. Entrepreneurs should assess their current capabilities and resources, identifying areas that require enhancement before scaling operations. This proactive approach helps prevent overextension, which can lead to burnout among staff and a decline in customer satisfaction. Engaging employees in this planning process can also foster a sense of ownership and commitment to the company's vision.

Financial management plays a pivotal role in sustainable growth. Entrepreneurs must ensure they have a solid financial foundation before pursuing aggressive expansion. This includes maintaining healthy cash, investing in technology, and optimizing operational efficiencies. By closely monitoring financial performance and making data-driven decisions, small business owners can avoid common pitfalls associated with rapid growth, such as excessive debt or inventory mismanagement. Regular financial reviews and adjustments to the growth strategy can help maintain balance and sustainability.

Another crucial element of sustainable growth is cultivating a strong company culture that supports innovation and adaptability. As businesses grow, the dynamics within the team can shift, potentially impacting morale and productivity. Leaders should prioritize open communication, professional development, and employee engagement to create an environment that encourages collaboration and creativity. This culture not only aids in retaining top talent but also empowers employees to contribute to the company's growth strategy, leading to innovative solutions and improved customer experiences.

Embracing corporate social responsibility (CSR) can enhance a business's reputation and contribute to sustainable growth. Entrepreneurs should consider how their operations affect the community and environment, striving to implement practices that promote sustainability. This can include sourcing materials responsibly, reducing waste, and engaging in community initiatives. By aligning business practices with ethical values, small business owners can attract a loyal customer base that values sustainability, ultimately leading to a more resilient and prosperous business model.

Chapter 11: Maintaining Work-Life Balance

THE IMPACT OF WORK-LIFE BALANCE ON SUCCESS

The concept of work-life balance has gained prominence in recent years, particularly among small business owners and entrepreneurs. This balance, often de ned as the ability to prioritize professional responsibilities and personal life, directly impacts an individual's overall success. When entrepreneurs achieve a harmonious balance, they enhance their well-being and increase their productivity and creativity, which are essential for driving business growth. The significance of this balance cannot be overstated; it serves as a foundation for sustainable success.

One of the most notable effects of work-life balance is improving mental health. Entrepreneurs often face high stress levels due to the demands of running a business. Stress can escalate when work consumes personal time, leading to burnout and decreased efficiency. By consciously setting boundaries and allocating time for individual interests and family, entrepreneurs can mitigate stress and foster a healthier mindset. This renewed mental clarity can stimulate innovative thinking and better decision-making, which are crucial for navigating the challenges of entrepreneurship.

Moreover, maintaining a work-life balance enhances professional and personal interpersonal relationships. Entrepreneurs prioritizing personal time often report stronger connections with family, friends, and colleagues. These relationships are vital, providing emotional support and networking opportunities that can lead to business growth. Engaging in social activities can spark new ideas and collaborations while reinforcing a sense of community that can be invaluable for small business owners. The ability to connect with others on a personal level often translates into improved customer relationships, which can directly impact sales and brand loyalty.

Additionally, a balanced lifestyle encourages better physical health, which is a critical component of overall success. Regular exercise, adequate sleep, and healthy eating habits often take a back seat when work demands increase. However, entrepreneurs who prioritize their health through a balanced approach are more likely to have the energy and stamina required to meet the rigorous demands of their businesses. Physical well-being enhances productivity and reduces the risk of illness, which can be particularly detrimental for those who are the primary drivers of their enterprises. In this regard, investing time in personal well-being is not just an option but a necessity for long-term success.

In conclusion, the impact of work-life balance on success for small business owners and entrepreneurs is profound. By recognizing the importance of this balance, entrepreneurs can create a more fulfilling and productive work environment. A commitment to work-life balance fosters mental and physical health, nurtures personal relationships, and supports professional growth. As entrepreneurs strive to think big and grow, embracing a balanced approach can set the stage for lasting success and innovation in their ventures.

STRATEGIES FOR TIME MANAGEMENT

Effective time management is crucial for small business owners and entrepreneurs aiming to maximize productivity and achieve growth. One foundational strategy is prioritization, distinguishing between urgent and important tasks. Using methods like the Eisenhower Matrix, entrepreneurs can categorize their responsibilities into four quadrants: urgent and important, important but not urgent, urgent but not necessary, and neither. This allows for a more explicit focus on high-impact activities that drive the business forward while minimizing time spent on less critical tasks.

Another vital approach is the implementation of the Pomodoro Technique, which encourages working in focused intervals, typically 25 minutes, followed by short breaks. This method enhances concentration and helps prevent burnout by allowing regular rest periods. Small business owners can adapt this technique by customizing the work intervals and breaks to suit their personal productivity rhythms. By adopting structured time blocks, entrepreneurs can create a sense of urgency and maintain motivation, leading to increased output and creativity.

Delegation plays a significant role in effective time management. Entrepreneurs often struggle with the desire to control every aspect of their business, which can lead to inefficiencies and overwhelm. By identifying tasks that can be delegated to team members or outsourced to freelancers, business owners can free up their time to focus on strategic initiatives. This empowers staff and fosters a collaborative environment that can enhance overall business performance. Establishing clear communication and expectations when delegating tasks is essential to ensure the work aligns with the business's goals.

Utilizing technology and productivity tools can significantly enhance entrepreneurs' time management. Project management software, calendar applications, and time-tracking apps allow business owners to organize tasks, set deadlines, and monitor progress. These resources can help streamline operations, reduce time spent on administrative tasks, and provide valuable insights into allocating time across various projects. By leveraging technology, entrepreneurs can create more efficient work that supports their growth objectives.

Finally, regular reflection and assessment of time management practices are essential for continuous improvement. Entrepreneurs should set aside time weekly or monthly to evaluate how effectively they manage their time. This includes reviewing accomplishments, identifying areas where time may have been wasted, and adjusting strategies as needed. By cultivating a habit of self-reflection, small business owners can stay aligned with their goals and make informed decisions that foster personal and professional growth, ultimately leading to a more sustainable and successful business.

PRIORITIZING SELF-CARE AND WELL-BEING

Prioritizing self-care and well-being is essential for small business owners and entrepreneurs who aspire to achieve sustained growth. The entrepreneurial journey is often fraught with stress, long hours, and the pressure to perform. As a result, many entrepreneurs sacrifice their health and well-being to pursue their business goals. However, neglecting self-care can lead to burnout and decreased productivity, ultimately hindering growth. By recognizing the importance of self-care, entrepreneurs can cultivate a mindset supporting personal and professional success.

Implementing a self-care routine is a luxury and necessary for maintaining high-performance levels. Entrepreneurs should identify activities that rejuvenate and energize them through physical exercise, mindfulness practices, or hobbies. Establishing a regular schedule for these activities can create a healthy boundary between work and personal life, allowing for a more balanced approach to daily responsibilities. By prioritizing these moments of self-care, business owners can enhance their focus and creativity, leading to better decision-making and problem-solving.

Mental health is a critical aspect of well-being that often goes overlooked in the entrepreneurial community. Entrepreneurs face unique challenges that can lead to feelings of isolation, anxiety, and depression. It is vital to foster an environment where mental health is openly discussed and prioritized. Entrepreneurs can benefit from seeking support through mentorship, networking groups, or professional counseling. By sharing experiences and challenges with peers, they can cultivate resilience and gain valuable insights that contribute to their personal growth and the health of their businesses.

Moreover, a healthy work-life balance is crucial for sustaining motivation and enthusiasm for one's business. Entrepreneurs should set clear boundaries regarding work hours and personal time, ensuring they dedicate time to family, friends, and personal interests outside of work. This balance prevents burnout and fosters creativity and innovation, which are essential for growth. When entrepreneurs take the time to recharge, they return to their businesses with renewed energy and fresh perspectives that can lead to breakthrough ideas.

Prioritizing self-care and well-being can serve as a powerful example for employees and other entrepreneurs within the community. Business leaders can create a culture encouraging others to follow suit by openly valuing personal health. This shift can lead to a more supportive and productive environment where everyone feels empowered to prioritize their well-being. Ultimately, investing in self-care is not just about individual benefits; it is a strategic approach that can drive the overall success of a business and foster a thriving entrepreneurial ecosystem.

Chapter 12: Conclusion: Your Journey Ahead

REFLECTING ON YOUR GROWTH JOURNEY

Reflecting on your growth journey is essential for small business owners and entrepreneurs seeking to master their entrepreneurial mindset. This process involves taking a step back to assess your experiences, challenges, and achievements over time. You can gain valuable personal and professional development insights by engaging in thoughtful reflection. This self-awareness fosters resilience and equips you with the knowledge to navigate future challenges more effectively.

As you embark on your growth journey, consider the pivotal moments shaping your entrepreneurial path. These moments include significant successes, failures, or unexpected opportunities that force you to adapt and innovate. Documenting these experiences can help you identify patterns in your decision-making and highlight the skills you have developed along the way. Understanding how you have responded to various situations can empower you to make more informed choices moving forward, ensuring that you continue to grow and evolve as a business owner.

Additionally, it is crucial to recognize the role of feedback in your growth journey. Engaging with mentors, peers, and customers can provide external perspectives that enrich your understanding of your business and its impact. Actively seeking constructive feedback allows you to identify areas for improvement and strengths you may have overlooked. By integrating this feedback into your reflection process, you can create a more comprehensive picture of your entrepreneurial journey and set actionable goals for the future.

Moreover, reflection is not just about looking back but also about envisioning your future. Use your reflections to set strategic goals that align with your long-term vision. This forward-thinking approach enables you to create a growth roadmap informed by experiences. You can maintain focus and motivation, even when faced with obstacles, by clearly articulating your aspirations and the steps needed to achieve them.

Finally, make reflection a regular practice in your entrepreneurial routine. Set aside dedicated time for this activity, whether through journaling, meditation, or discussions with trusted advisors. Consistent reflection helps to reinforce the lessons learned and keeps your growth mindset active. Embracing this habit allows you to continuously review your strategies, celebrate your achievements, and prepare for the challenges, ultimately leading to a more prosperous and fulfilling entrepreneurial journey.

STAYING COMMITTED TO YOUR VISION

Staying committed to your vision is a fundamental aspect of entrepreneurial success. For small business owners and entrepreneurs, the journey is often fraught with challenges that can easily divert focus from long-term goals. The ability to maintain a steadfast commitment to your vision requires not only passion but also a strategic approach to navigating obstacles. Clear articulation of your vision is a guiding star, helping you navigate uncertainties and maintaining the motivation to push forward.

To enhance your commitment, revisiting and renewing your vision regularly is essential. As markets evolve and consumer needs change, so should your vision adapt. This process involves critically evaluating your initial goals and determining whether they still resonate with your current aspirations and the realities of your business environment. Engaging in this reflective practice reinforces your commitment and ensures that your vision remains relevant and inspiring, encouraging you to strive for growth while fostering resilience against setbacks.

Moreover, surrounding yourself with a supportive network can significantly bolster your commitment to your vision. This network may include mentors, fellow entrepreneurs, or employees who share your passion. Collaboration and open communication within this circle can provide valuable insights and encouragement, helping you focus on your goals. The power of shared experiences and collective problem-solving can reignite your passion during tough times, reminding you of the purpose behind your entrepreneurial journey.

Accountability is another critical component in maintaining your commitment. Establishing measurable milestones and setting deadlines not only helps to track your progress but also reinforces your resolve. You create a structured framework that encourages discipline and consistency when you hold yourself accountable. Regularly reviewing these milestones allows you to celebrate achievements and reassess strategies, ensuring that your vision remains at the forefront of your daily activities and decision-making processes.

Embracing a growth mindset is vital for sustaining your commitment to your vision. This mindset encourages you to view challenges as opportunities for learning and development rather than insurmountable obstacles. You cultivate an environment where innovation thrives by fostering a culture of adaptability and resilience within yourself and your business. This adaptability is key to staying aligned with your vision, as it empowers you to pivot when necessary while keeping the ultimate goal in sight. In doing so, you commit to your vision and inspire those around you to do the same, creating a powerful momentum for success.

EMBRACING THE ENTREPRENEURIAL ADVENTURE

Embracing the entrepreneurial adventure involves recognizing the journey as a dynamic process of growth and learning. Many small business owners start with a vision, an idea that sparks their passion. However, the true essence of entrepreneurship lies not just in the conception of a business but in the continuous evolution of that concept. Entrepreneurs must remain adaptable and ready to pivot in response to market changes, customer feedback, and personal insights. This mindset fosters resilience, allowing business owners to face challenges head-on and view setbacks as opportunities for learning rather than insurmountable barriers.

At the core of the entrepreneurial adventure is the willingness to take risks. Entrepreneurs must be comfortable with uncertainty, understanding that risk is inherent in starting and running a business. This does not mean acting recklessly; it involves making informed decisions based on data, research, and intuition. By embracing calculated risks, small business owners can explore new markets, innovate products, and adopt strategies that may lead to significant growth. Each risk is a step toward a greater understanding and mastery of the entrepreneurial landscape.

Networking and collaboration are also essential components of the entrepreneurial journey. Building relationships with other entrepreneurs, mentors, and industry professionals provides valuable insights and support. Engaging with a community of like-minded individuals fosters a culture of sharing, where experiences and resources can be exchanged. This collaborative spirit enhances personal growth and can lead to business opportunities that might not have been accessible in isolation. Entrepreneurs actively seeking partnerships and alliances position themselves for more tremendous success.

Another critical aspect of embracing the entrepreneurial adventure is the importance of continuous learning. The business world constantly evolves and is influenced by technological advancements, consumer behavior shifts, and economic changes. Entrepreneurs must commit to lifelong learning through formal education, workshops, or self-directed study. This commitment allows them to stay ahead of trends, improve their skills, and make informed decisions that drive growth. By fostering a learning mindset, small business owners can better navigate the complexities of their industries and remain competitive.

Cultivating a strong sense of purpose is vital in the entrepreneurial journey. A clear vision and mission inspire entrepreneurs to push through challenges and maintain focus on their goals. This sense of purpose drives personal motivation and resonates with customers and employees, creating a shared understanding of commitment to the business. By aligning their actions with their core values, entrepreneurs can build a brand that reflects authenticity and attracts loyal customers. Embracing the entrepreneurial adventure means embracing this purpose-driven approach, leading to personal fulfillment and business success.

About the Author

Samuel Theo Yamthe, the Author of this book, is an entrepreneur, investment adviser, and business consultant with over 22 years of experience in business. As a seasoned catalyst for transformation, Investment Adviser, Business Consultant, and Entrepreneur, Samuel explains how to deliver results, turning visions into reality. His profound expertise is backed by his academic journey as a Doctoral Candidate in Global Business Management and Leadership. In a world where change is the only constant, having insight from a trusted expert like Samuel is not just an option but a necessity. His insights and strategies in the book are designed to help navigate today's complex business landscape, ensuring businesses survives and thrives. Samuel's holistic approach combines deep industry knowledge with practical information that can be tailored to each business's unique needs.